Patricio León C.

# Rhapsody of Strings under the Moonlight

Bedtime Poems & Stories

## @Rhapsody of Strings under the Moonlight

Author: **Patricio León C.**
Editing & Proofreading: **Olga Agustín**
Design and layout: **Lissa V. Pérez Gómez, MsC**
Illustrative Artwork: **Miguel Lendor "Papachín"**
Publisher: **Producciones León**



For permission requests, contact: **Patricio León**
E-mail: **patricioleoncruz@gmail.com**

# Rhapsody of Strings under the Moonlight

Bedtime Poems & Stories

Patricio León C.

# Índice


Patricio León.................................................................7

Impressions on Rhapsody of Strings under the Moonlight.................9

First String: **Our cat & the neighbors**.................15

Second String: **Hidden confesion**.....................21

Third String: **Epiphany moon**.......................27

Fourth String: **Invasion of the moon**..................31

Fifth String: **Burglars**..............................39

Sixth String: **Feral**................................43

Seventh String: **I don't want to**....................51

Eighth String: **The note**...........................57

Ninth String: **Interstellar rising**....................63

Tenth String: **In lust with the moon**................71

Eleventh String: **Mise en scene, interrupted**.........75

Twelfth String: **The cohorts**.......................79

Thirteenth String: **Troika**.........................85

Fourteenth String: **Killing the moon**................91

Fifteenth String: **Tamed**.........................97

Sixteenth String: **Emasculating nature**..............103

# Patricio León
@PatricioLeonC

Dramatic actor, musician, narrator, poet
and educator.

Passionate about art, education in science and child education.

He has certifications in **Applied Neurosciences in Education for early childhood** from the **Instituto de Neuropsicologia RD**, 2015; **Theatre Pedagody** from the **National Theatre Eduardo Brito**, **Ministry of Culture**, 2014, and **Leadership** from the **Carnegie Dale School**, 2015.

He has two bachelors degrees, the first one in **Social Communications** and the second one in **Pedagogy**, both from the **Autonomous University of Santo Domingo**, as well as a masters in **Corporate Management** from **UNAPEC**.

From the Ministry of Education of the Dominican Republic he has directed, participated and accompanied several **Science, Childhood and Value Education** programs and projects.

Of his independent productions stand out: "**Book Compendio de Comunicacion Moderna**", 2011; educational and cinematographic documentary "**Teatrografia Dominicana**", 2015; audiovisual production "**Coleccion Clásica de Lectura de Literatura Universal**", 2017; "**Guide for Pedagogical Technical Evaluation of Children's and Young People's Literature**", 2019, children's and youth's literary book accompanied with neuroeduactional guide "**Tales from Vennet**", 2020 y and the book "**The Game: dialogued reflections of a neuroeducateur**", 2021.

As a dramatic actor, the classics are his specialty. Patricio León has interpreted iconic characters from plays such as: "**Waiting for Godot**" of Samuel Beckett, "**The House of Bernarda Alba**" of Federico García Lorca, "**The Tunnel**" of Ernesto Sábato, " **The Barrel of Amontillado**" of Edgar Allan Poe, "**The Toothbrush**" of Jorge Díaz and "**The Autopsy**" of Enrique Buenaventura, amongst many others.

# Impressions on Rhapsody of Strings under the Moonlight

Perhaps only Patricio León, - in whom narrator, musician, poet, and actor converge altogether- could write Rhapsody of Strings under the Moonlight. Bedtime Poems & Stories. A work whose title foreshadows the blend of practices and styles inspired by epic, theater, and music, from the great poems of Homer till present-day, and which amid the 19th century became very popular during musical romanticism, with the rhapsodies of Franz Liszt (1811-1886) and the Hungarian dances of Johannes Brahms (1833-1897), two of its highest representatives, in which themed contrasts and formal freedom are prevalent.

Fragmented into sixteen excerpts, stories or scenes, this brief work by León focuses on the breakup of a couple of unnamed lovers without explicit gender, swept away by the gale of passion and desire, with the moon as their sole spectator and accomplice, and the presence of a cat that serves as witness to the impulses of a love that is hopelessly undone in the misunderstanding of bodies scorched by the fire of the sexes. The work is a heartbroken cry of a lonely, proud individual, overpowered by his own ego in the face of the loss and abandonment of the one who filled his days. And on the other end, silence, and emptiness as the only response.

With a prose fluid with poetic intent, where occasionally an intertextual reference slips in ("Alberti's mistaken dove", he says in "Hidden Confession"), León's work proclaims in each subtitle the outbursts of a relationship doomed to an estrangement that would seem irreconcilable. But it also bears witness to the carnal and transgressive nature of an overwhelming eroticism. In "Lunar Subversion", we read: "Don't blame my eyes, for they are subjects; they pursue your sex, and they don't... they don't shame me. It is but an unspeakable attraction".

In a key book on the subject, The Double Flame: Love and Eroticism (1994), Octavio Paz (1914-1998) wrote that eroticism is "first and foremost a thirst for otherness", while love "is an attraction to a unique person: to a body and a soul. Love is choice; eroticism, acceptance". In León's book, according to the evidence offered by his own words, the balance between love and eroticism tips towards the latter, weighed down by the overwhelming burden of desire, in an absolute deification of the body and its sensory drives.

The whole book is imbued with a deeply moving sentimental tone that strikes with the force of a desperate ritornello. It is, in short, an initiatory journey into the deceptive labyrinths of heartbreak, in painful texts that the author himself, a young artist of versatile talent, will undoubtedly take up again to tread new paths.

**José Alcántara Almánzar**

# Our cat
# & the neighbors

First String

Our cat's meow spells your name loud and clear.
I've asked the neighbors if they understand it, but
they -who know nothing of love, longing, and desire
with frenzy- respond that they don't understand,
and that if I do, it's because I'm crazy…. But
they're the crazy ones! I clearly hear your name!

Me? Crazy? Yes, that is also true; but not because of
the same illness: theirs is the incapacity to recognize
love; and mine, the comical drama of a love no
more.

Yes, I'm crazy! But not crazier than the cat. I see it
in its lost gaze, distant in time and space. I'm more
"normally" crazy; it's like I'm crazy, but because
I've bound myself to you.

But the cat? Wow! He doesn't eat, and sleeps by the
porch; but he doesn't sleep, he wanders around. It
guards an entrance, waiting for someone who will
no longer come through the door, and I've said
thousandfold… And yet, it remains hopeful in a
way I've never seen before. It aches me greatly to
see him like this, hence why I've decided to join him
in his standby; the difference lies in me knowing

for a fact that you won't be back. Can you tell the difference? At least, I'm aware, but the cat? I don't know.

A chronic pain binds me to our cat, spawned from the same emotional knot. I just think he hasn't understood that you've got a new love, that you need your space, and time to live that moment, and that we need to respect your happiness. But how can your miserable happiness cause such deep sorrow in our cat?

Sometimes I wonder, and I have my theories written down, that our cat meows your name, because he thinks I do no effort to reach you. His intuition that I miss you is correct; he then grabs the bull by the horns and calls out to you…. But he's wrong; he ignores that my calls for you are stronger than his meow; and that my search for you goes beyond waiting for you by the doorway.

I cannot fathom how our neighbors don't understand our cat when -whereby his meow- he calls out to you loud and clear.

It is so obvious! Like when the coffee comes to a
boil, and infuses ipso facto with its freshly brewed
aroma, and everyone can immediately tell. They
haven't a clue what it is to love, to miss and to
yearn.

Every day, our cat and I grow more alike.
Perhaps it is because we've become inseparable,
even though he knows I never wanted him here
-at home- and was utterly against it until you
convinced me otherwise: You subtly played me
into agreeing; that crazy night; a trap you subdued
me into, as we enjoyed the night with our bodies
becoming one.

At dawn, as the moon was vanished by the sun, I
promised our cat he'd never need to learn another
name, and that I'd rather meow your name by
his side; by the porch, every night, despite our
neighbors never coming to terms.

# Hidden confesion

Second String

I confess I love you

I bore witness of the aura within you, and I know
no one else but I can see it. If you only knew how I
see it, you'd fly your way back to me.

But you've gone in the opposite way, like the stray
dove in Alberti's writings; and I am here, taming my
longing and the sadness of not having you near me,
my heart sending you a sign, -strong signs-, though
they seem not to reach you.

How is it that without knowing, you alter the
cogency of my dreams?
I only wish you'd knew without me having to tell
you

I can hide my emotion upon the mere sight of you,
though its expression underlies in the vanishing of
your presence, lieu of my eternal innocence.

I wish I were, in the very least, the butt of your dead
cigarette.

I would then have some proof of having tasted your
lips.

*24*

Let me -at least- gaze upon you. I'm good at gazing.
I watch in curt manner, without trace to give
away my longing for your lips to caress mine; still,
consuming the whim stirring my sensorium, thus
hiding my love for you.

But dawn comes and reveals all, and it is wherefore
impossible for you to not know I love you, before
saying the words.

# Epiphany moon

Third String

I feel an overwhelming sadness. I don't know why.

I only know I want to cry, until I rid myself of all this sadness I carry, but alas, I am unable to cry. I don't know why.

I only know that I wish I could express every feeling I bear inside, but I am alas incapable of expressing myself. I don't know why.

I only know that I'd love to dance to the most wistful and sad music ever composed, but I find myself too clumsy to dance.

I know what's happening to me. The moon has done it yet again: I'm just especially………

# Invasion
# of the moon

Fourth String

I woke up in good spirits today, humming to the
tune of a song, I'd long since forgotten, whilst
whistling another; as I performed my day-to-day
chores, folding laundry, cleaning the floor, I even ran
into a chore among my most unliked: making the
bed.

And, though I dislike it immensely, I began getting
it done without protest; I looked, while whistling,
the ends of the sheet, and got lost. It was quite
a rumpled sight, more than usual. Everything
changed. That miserliness the sun greeted me with,
and the gentle blow of tranquility, no longer joined
me; there was something strange in my bed and
knowing that benumbed me.

I slowly examined all crease marks in that strange
body, and it came to me: "someone -other than me-
was in the bed last night. Was it you? Of course,
it was you! Who else? But I'd rather give you the
benefit of the doubt.

Did you return? A-N-S-W-E-R ME!! Was my
restraining order not enough, signed and sealed by
your heart? I was already getting used to my routine
without you. Come on! A-N-S-W-E-R M-E!!

What if it is my mind playing tricks and you
haven't -in fact- been here? I only recall a deep and
beautiful slumber. Let's do a play-by-play of last
night:

1.  I smell the bed like a dog sniffing for drugs,
    and yes: it smells like you; that unmistakable
    and fascinating blend of lavender fields and
    cedarwood. Oh! Such is this a whyfor flawed,
    to the point of rebuttal in any trial. Besides,
    for such a long time I carried your scent in me,
    sensing it even in the most putrid venues, and
    you were nowhere near.

2.  I gaze with suspicion and distrust the crease
    marks patterned in the sheets and yet remain
    in the bed, and yes: these are the same crease
    marks and vestiges we left upon becoming one
    in the night, but such proof lacks force.

3. It's best I call you to ask for your alibi. Of course, this should've been my starting point. Of course, it's always good to have a confessed culprit, that solves the case without major setbacks. But I can't, I swore to myself I'd ever dial your number, and I'm a man of my word! This case I will sort without your help, as I've done so far since the day you called on me no more.

4. Lastly, I check, aghast, my clothes, searching for signs, those signs that could attest to the climax of those games once played, and yes: they are there. However, this neither proves you visiting my bed; I could have been indeed cavorting with, but without you, and oblivious to that fact….

Are you back? ¡A-N-S-W-E-R -M-E! Is it not enough the change of heart of my feelings, and my stronger guard – doubled as in a boardgame match? Come on! A-N-S-W-E-R M-E!!

You know what? Don't answer! Now that I think about it, I've ruled out the first and most irrefutable of proof: the whistling, that calming sound that joined me every waking moment -now gone-, has given me the answer I sought. Horror! We have not moved on! You were here. It's not my mind playing tricks on me.

I feel rage because you tamper not only my mind and spirit, but, you are in cohorts with the Moon and Morpheus so that I am left helpless, and yes, it is violence, you abuse me, for you haven't my permission, as always, like those myriad stolen wonderful autumn nights.

Unbelievable, you were here, again! Again! I haven't got the energy to change the sheets, nor make the bed.

I want to whistle again in the morning, regardless of my need to tend the bed. Unlock my guard with your kisses, even if you best me – like always- in boardgames, lift the restraining order, because all I want is to whistle again in the morning.

# Burglars

Fifth String

Someone else has deprived me of the privilege
to gaze at you while dreaming, and I strip them of
your breath and deepest sighs.

Today, like yesterday, I want you not just for the
night -which is fine- and how I enjoy it so! I want us
to slowly bid the moon farewell and salute the sun.

We were doing so well without having met! I was
so set on meeting you, and you, in your permitted
life…. A farse, but a permitted one.

I don't want to hide our love. I want, in some way,
for us to create a way to be together: at night, at
daytime, under the rain, at dawn, in public, and
alone; but together.

I don't wish to be without you. I want you for
myself.

# Feral

Sixth String

I'm like a beast licking its wounds, far from sight.

You leave tonight my love. You announced it a week ago, and your actions from last night relish this before my hurt and prideful heart. And me? As if nothing happened; stoic, continuing with my day's agenda.

Since dawn, I've kept busy with my day-to-day affairs. I fixed breakfast for two, as usual; nothing special. Breakfast was more ordinary than usual; everything well set, no variance whatsoever, so you see that I moved on, living my life.

In the bathroom, behind closed doors, I rehearse my smile, the usual smile, no more nor less intense; I don't dress in neither black nor red, but in blue. Greetings? The necessary ones, the usual ones, so that neighbors, acquaintances, and colleagues at work don't notice how broken I feel with the news of your desertion, which is old news.

The day goes by slowly, amid a bedlam that
unhinges me within, expecting for the expected not
to come. And then comes the night.

I come home, our home; and there you are.
You packed all your things and have exerted the
unrequested kindness of waiting to say "goodbye".
Your eyes, -and even your body- scream that you
don't want to leave… you want me to stop you. We
look at each other's eyes.

And me? Here: still, unafraid, firm; with a defying
gaze and yet, apparently calm.

I hope that in the time spent together, you learned
to understand me, because if you look into my eyes
and at my face, you'll see how they reflect my ego,
and my uncompromising attitude where "nothing
is going on", and you will leave even sooner; for
you see my love, my eyes are not the windows to
my soul; it takes digging deeper to figure me out.
However, if you can -in fact- see me with your
heart, you'll see I bend, that I'm begging you to stay
and forgive me. Take a few seconds, my love, t oread
into me, because if you judge by the first impression,
you'll be gone, and we will be done… I'll be done.

Your tears come out, and how I wish I
could taste them, lick them dry. Mine? They
remain well-hidden, they won't show. They
are contained, at least until I bolt the door
with all three locks, following your departure;
upon closing the blinds; and after turning
off the lights, succumb into a silent but deep
mourning… so deep, like all the ideas I wish
to share with you just now when you decide to
leave.

The second reading, my love! My beautiful
love! My only love! The second reading. I trust
you aren't a simpleton too stubborn so as not
to take a second look. Spare this inevitable pain
and grant me the joy of remaining by your side

The second, please! The second! Because if
you choose the first, you'll destroy me forever
without any knowledge thereof. It will be after
you've gone, with the night upon, alongside the
moon, witness each night to our love, that I'll
find solace and let my soul pour.

Tasteless tears will shed, announcing their expel, and they won't shed from my eyes. You know me well, my love, and you know they are deep; they shed from my essence, where I hope you were able to explore and understand my need for you to stay and forgive this ego -an ego only YOU can forgive-.

No matter what: if you cross that door, that's it. I swear! I'm not a haphazard man. In matters like this, I'm a feral beast, harboring ill will. I don't know its antonym. Cross that door and…..that door is -right now- the only thing that could save us.

If you stay, I swear the tip of my tongue will set off on a journey; I will tread softly and loosely in each of your sanctuaries, conveying my message. Stay, my love. Let's stay! Let's stay for us. Let's forgive and forget, and rebuild trust and this love, a flame still alive and threatened to run extinct by that menacing door.

But, if you insist on leaving, then leave! Just leave
already, no hesitation. The tears will be soon
upon my eyes, wishing to break down the barriers
between reason and my soul. Stay, or go, because
they're almost here.

Run, my love! For I am feral, a beast licking its
wounds, but alone, far from sight. Run, my love!
For the tears are soon upon, like a volcano close to
erosion, unstoppable, not even by your choosing to
stay.

Run, my love; run, because my tears run hot.

# I don't want to

Seventh String

I don't want my first thoughts to be about you; in fact, I condemn myself. And yet, I don't know how to command my mind, - which is more yours than it ever was mine, and untamable as it is, it refuses to let me forget you.

I'm enraged because I assume you never think of me throughout the day. It needn't be at dawn, I can settle for when fresh brewed coffee touches your lips, or the wine coming to life in your mouth.

And when I say "I assume" you never think about me, it's because, if you did in the very least, it would tear down the walls between the moon and I at dusk. Come on! You don't need to say you think of me, a single hint or sign would do, to make me continue creating -in an ideal and parallel universe- moments for us two.

I swear I command every fiber of my being not to think of you, and then, a faint, but probing trave of hope, tells me that perhaps you do; and deciding not to think of you only deepens the rift between us.

Please! At least one sign……

# The note

Eighth String

You needed an excuse to explain yourself
and, since you couldn't find one, you fled…
leaving only a farewell note.

But it isn't a note, it is a dagger vilely
sharpened by a poisonous rock.

The moon wandered off, and I was unable to
tear up your farewell note, I chose to learn it
word for word and memorize it by heart.

My eyes itch in the wee hours of the morning.
I take them for a walk to appease their ardor,
but a heavy and disturbing presence, glued to
me, pulls at them.

I, such a Penelope; and you and the moon, are
Don Juan.

There are days when I take the letter out of
the house and put it in the mailbox, as if it had
not come to me, and I imagine that you have
not left. I summon memories that turn back
time and bring you to me.

And again, it begins to get dark, and a row of desires multiplies; I feel a certain uneasiness not having the pleasure of making them come true. I have a well full of desires and they all have to do with you.

I don't want another touch; I don't want another body. Close doors. Turn off the lights. I'm all alone and dry. The most moisturizing creams make cracks in my acidic, arid, and lonely skin.

While others live, I remain wounded in an agony that finds no end.

I want to dance with you again, but it's not dancing that interests me, it's dancing with you.

Come back, I'll forgive you again.

# Interstellar rising

Ninth String

Don't blame my eyes, they are minions;
they go after your sex, and no... they don't
embarrass me. It is an ineffable attraction.

I imagine you closer and closer, as if between
my sex and yours there were a magnetism
dominated by my mind. That place so neat
and complex that seduces you to me, without
you being aware.

Don't blame my eyes, they are minions;
they go behind you, when you turn around,
focusing on that part that I suspect with
certainty accommodates me and crave to have.

I have an urge to encircle your waist; to
squeeze you and glue my sex to yours, in a
greeting that would only be the entrance to
give way to a score I have in my head and
couldn't perform with anyone else, because
it's in my head. And what is in my head, only
I know; and, on this exclusive occasion, I am
willing to share it with you.

Don't blame my eyes, they are minions; they only
want to lead you to me so that, when you reach the
corner of the dark corridor, they appear by surprise.
There, to corner you behind the purple partition,
without you being able to escape; and to grope, with
intention, your instruments, in the chiaroscuro of
said corner.

And yes, I know that you have the strength to
escape, and you don't do it....

I start the first notes shown in the score and you
pretend not to want to play the first voice, which
was written exclusively for you; you shy away and
then I frustrate your escape. I play the first notes
again, and you shy away again. And I repeat the
intro again, and then you seem to enter my mind
and take possession of the score I have composed;
and then you begin to play the first voice, in
the most sublime and most perfect way that the
composer can envision.

The score marches on swiftly. Your entrances and
accents become the highlights of the performance.

We saunder from tempo to tempo. And I fill my mouth with the flavors of your body; my ears, with your breath; and my mind, with your being. Our hearts beat beautifully dissonant with crescendi and decrescendi; and your sex is all mine, and mine moves in your paradise... the one that from the beginning could not be banished from my sight.

I notice - strangely - that you speed up the passage from one note to the next, from one beat to another. You do not respect the silences marked in the score. You run. You turn whites into crotchets; crotchets into eighth notes; eighth notes into sixteenth notes.... And I, who am the composer, know that the inevitable end of my composition is near, the one you have already altered with your allegros and vivace. You approach the staccato and, when we almost reach the imminent last bar, rearguard! da capo!

I don't want to disengage my sex from yours, that sacred place where it lies so comfortably. I apply an adagio, but you return to the allegro, indomitable this time. The snare drums of the already inevitable end appear sooner than expected, and I apply my last resort: a ritardando and a fermata; and then, only then, the music ends.

We walked away in opposite directions and only
I turned my face to look for your sex, which was
already far away. The purple partition and this
corner will never be the same again: silent witnesses
of our performance.

Can you be sad and happy at the same time? I am
sad, but I can die right now. My body tastes like you.
I had you, I was happy.

Now do you understand that my eyes were not to
blame?

# In lust
# with the moon

Tenth String

Gray, colorless days, without highs or lows; and then, without warning, that fortuitous, fleeting, and vague rendezvous. Then, I returned to believe, to dream and to hope.

My hopes were renewed and, encouraged by the silence of my fears and excited by your arrival, I danced celebrating your arrival.

Last night, last night I thought of you again and sank into myself. I felt a "je ne sais quoi", a kind of unfathomable sadness, because you are not coming; a rush, as if my body was souring; an urgency for you to finally come and fill my dark holes.

My mysterious heart has closed passages, waiting for you to come, with your magic, and to vanish high walls.

I wait for you. The written reasons are in my heart, with an alphabet legible only to me; for I don't want anyone to suspect that I've been waiting for you for a long time, until you arrive, I know for sure and then I can shout that I've been waiting for you.

# Mise en scene, interrupted

Eleventh String

I feel rage knowing that I think of you and immediately your partner appears in the center proscenium arch, as if hidden in a side of the stage; attentive to my thoughts, to make an entrance and ruin the scene for me.

And, when I command him to leave, he obediently goes out of the way, but takes you in his arms. Then, the presentation without you is meaningless.

And the ruler shouts, "Drop the curtain!".

# The cohorts

Twelfth String

The unworthy moon has a game, and it is with me. When I go out to face it, it hides between the sheets, it sneaks mockingly out of my solitude.

I know I'm awake, but I'm afraid to open my eyes and realize you're not there, that you're gone, that it was a dream… the recurring one, but a dream.

It dawned again without you. The moon has done it to me again: it took you along.

And isn't waking up supposed to make nightmares fade away so one can see clearly? I don't see clearly. You're not still here.

I'm awake, afraid to open my eyes and realize the moon isn't here either.

Shouldn't nightmares have a sweet moment to appreciate the horror in them? You know…. that yin and yang thing.

If I open my eyes, to gaze at the morning, I will collide head-on with an atrocious reality: I've lost twice over. Too bad I'm not a god to have stopped time and prevented flight.

The brilliant understudy told me that you were
going together; embraced like intimate partners,
always together.

I should not have given in to the seductive charms
of the moon, it played dirty tricks on me again! Had
I known in time, I would have tied the moon's lips,
your foot and my heart, from the leg of the bed.

I refuse to open my eyes and face a reality, which
is foreign; a truth, which is neither mine; and a
loneliness, which I wish to be interrupt by the spell
of the moon and your return.

I have begged the understudy to leave. "Send me
the moon!", I said, squeezing my eyes shut.

I am sure we will meet again; the moon will bring
you to me.

You will come back to me; I know you will come
back.

# Troika

Thirteenth String

I haven't heard from the moon for a long time.
One night, after your departure, the phone rang,
and it was her; it was the last time she spoke to me
and reproached me for ignoring you.

You told her, on purpose, the words I'd spoken to
you at our last meeting; those hurtful words that
provoked your stupor and absolute perplexity; those
hurtful words that I can no longer take back.

I didn't want to talk about those words with the
moon, but she insisted; she hammered them at me.
She would tell me again and again:

—You shouldn't have said those words to her! Now
you are paying the price for your free expression.

—I know! I know! Don't you think I know?

—And don't you dare answer. Don't remind me of
them anymore; they're stuck in my memory, like a
stain that won't go away, that's there forever.

I can't breathe without running them over my heart
every night.

I sent her away, she hung up and there was a
long silence that, to this day, still clangors.

Three years have passed since the event and
none of the three of us have dared to return to
her words.

I remember the first time I connected with the
moon. It was an autumn night. I saw it as never
before, full of music. My motionless pupils
danced. The complicity was so great that a
concerned, but very wise voice warned me: "Be
careful, it dazzles!

I did not realize, until much later, that her
beauty was dangerous; and that, after that
encounter, I would never be the same again.

I understood love, once and forever... and I
waited for it.

Years passed until a current of air, which
was not typical of that season of the year,
accompanied by sweet melodies, appeared; and
with it, you.

I met you, and I reconnected with that autumn moon; then, I understood what was happening.

Today everything looks so colorless... devoid of you... I am left with only nostalgia, and a blind present, absent of music and future.

I am in hell. I met the moon and tasted your body: the only paradise that exists, I was there!

At least give me back the moon. My animosity is with you, not with her; and, by the way, when you bring her back, embrace me if you can.

Don't you see, don't you realize that the moon has our initials written on it? And that, without it, I can't sleep.

Let the moon come, to dream you again as it does every night; and then, come, kiss me, and run away... if you can.

# Killing
# the moon

Fourteenth String

A.– **H**elp!
B.– Shh!


A.– Help!
B.– Shh!


A.– Help!
B.– Shh!


A.– Help! It's just that…
B.– It isn't safe.


A.– But you promised…
B.– Not yet.


A.– I saw it
B.– Clearly?


A.– Clearer than ever before.
B.– But not enough.

A.– I glimpsed

B.– And? did you see it?

94

A.– Yes, I saw it

B.– You swear you did? Can you swear it?


B.– Help!

A.– Shh!


B.– Help!

A.– Shh!


B.– Help!

A.– Shh!

# Tamed

Fifteenth String

I've been feeling like a stranger in the company
of your people for a long time. I don't fit in. And, if
I keep forcing myself to fit into your world -which
is impossible because my nature exempts me-, I
will atrophy my essence and I will no longer be me;
and, above all things, I want to be me, if only for a
moment. Late? I don't know, I want to find out for
myself.

With yours I annihilated myself; and now that
my eyes are beginning to be born, I prefer to lose
everything that is not mine. My wings are atrophied,
I know, but I have my feet willing and restless to go
as far as I can, without you and yours.

Yes, I may die on the way, and I don't care. I'm
already so dead, like a hostage sentenced to death
who has given up hope of being rescued.

A few days ago, I saw a jet-black stallion....
beautiful. With singular elegance, he saw me and
galloped off steadily, sure of what he was doing, he
was chasing the moon. I followed him with my eyes
as far as I could, and he got lost; I felt that he was
rescuing me and showing me the way.

I don't know if I can get as far as the horse or if I can get lost with the moon, to look for me and find myself face to face, naked alongside it, because the internal fracture that afflicts me, limits me. My wings do not open, and my tired legs no longer respond to my commands; they will move only with the breath of my heart.

I am tired and mistakenly tamed, but my heart is fresh and lifeless. I'll ask the moon if it will do any good to protect a heart with no thorns, no scars.

Will it hurt? I don't know. But I'd rather the pain than have my heart, -brand new and lifeless- die without knowing the moon's answer.

Here I am, moon, still breathing.

# Emasculating nature

Sixteenth String

I see you, even from afar. My eyes are not always
with me; when I want, they move with my soul.

I too go against my nature. I have bound myself
so as not to break everything in my path and drag
myself to meet you.

We are anti-nature; and our ecosystem suffers,
weakens.

On my end, I have tried to drown the pain and
these feelings, which silence me, and it has been in
vain; I have thrown them into the air, to be carried
away by the wind, but it has been useless: they come
back, they torment me, they walk with me, and I
know they will not go away.

I see you, even from afar, and I ask myself, "How
will you bear it?".

If one day you are suddenly attacked by a piercing
pain that pierces your soul and you think that
you cannot go on without me, nor I without you,
here is a decalogue so that this life passes quickly
and unnoticed; and our separation, imposed and
emasculating, hurts less:

1. Don't recite that poem by Lope de Vega.

2. Don't pause the movies, to psychoanalyze the characters.

3. Forget about bringing her roses, especially yellow ones.

4. If he talks a lot and overwhelms you with a verbiage, don't silence him with your kisses, as you did with me, invent another strategy.

5. Do not dare to fill his existential uncertainties, with your logical certainties.

6. Don't wink at him when he argues with you, to disarm him with that smile of yours, perfect, that can only be seen on your face.

7. Avoid, at all costs, to pass near our special places.

8. If at any time we coincide, don't allow our glances to cross, even if the invisible magnet is stronger; turn your head, conceal your gaze, until I pass.

9.  Tell no one about us, they would die of envy;
    they would not bear the greatness of our love
    and would try to defame and destroy our
    memory, let us keep it to ourselves; and 2.

10. Pray with faith, if possible, on our knees, so
    that our thoughts do not cross and create, with
    their indestructible force: the way to break this
    decalogue and turn it into an anti-decalogue;
    and to make it possible for the moon to shine
    again, the river to resume its flowing course and
    at dawn the little birds to resume their chirping.

Love, flee from us. Do not try, under any
circumstance, even if you think of me from afar and
succumb, to refute this Decalogue; for only if you
take it to the letter, will you succeed, some sad and
revolutionary day, in not thinking of me.

As far as I am concerned, that day will never come.

OTHER TITLES
by Patricio León

**Tales from Vennet**
Anthology of children's and youth stories
with neurodidactic guidance.

**The game: reflections in dialogue
from a neuroeducational artist**
A work that addresses the game
as a strategy par excellence
for formal and non-formal education,
through which it breaks paradigms,
brings strategies and shares your vision
on the educational task.

**Modern Communication Compendium**
Compilation of essays on communication,
globalization and society.